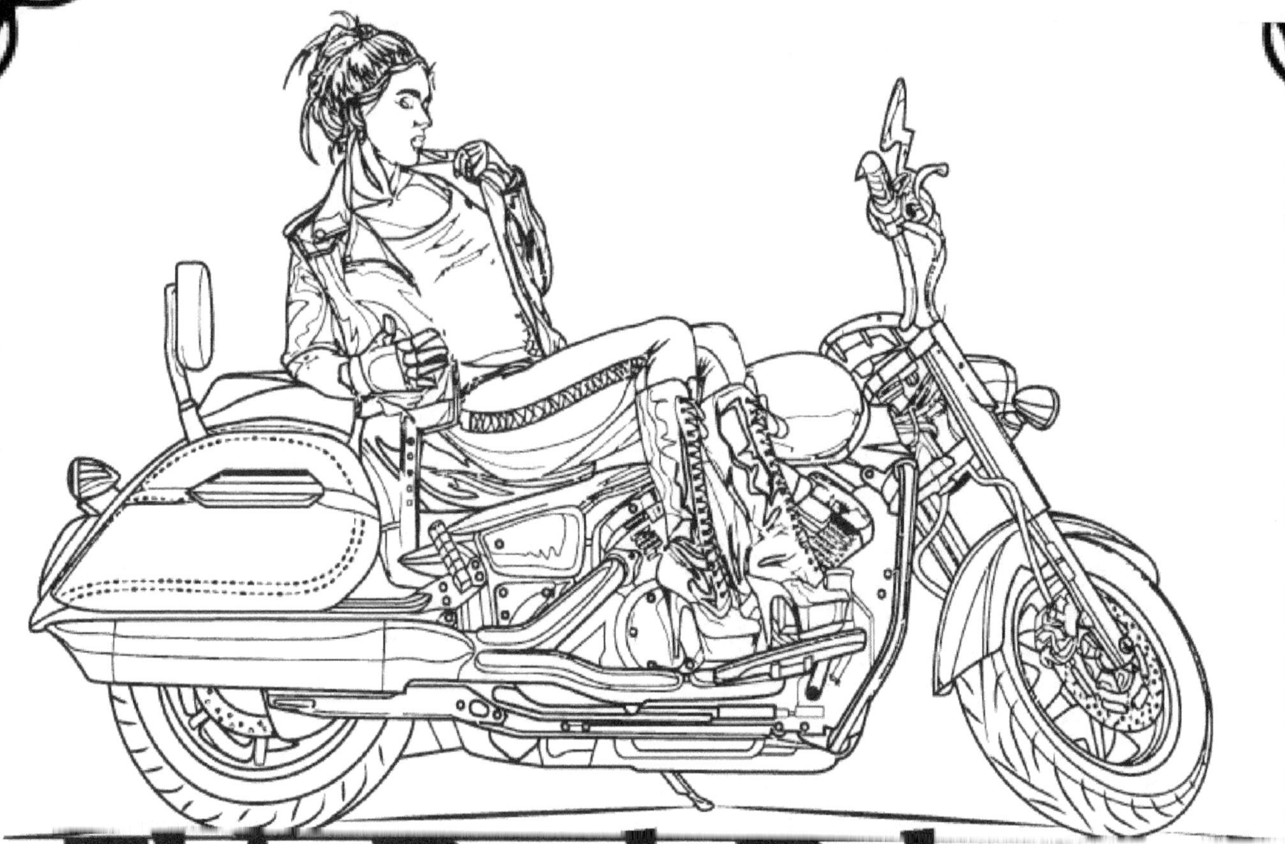

This Book Belongs

To

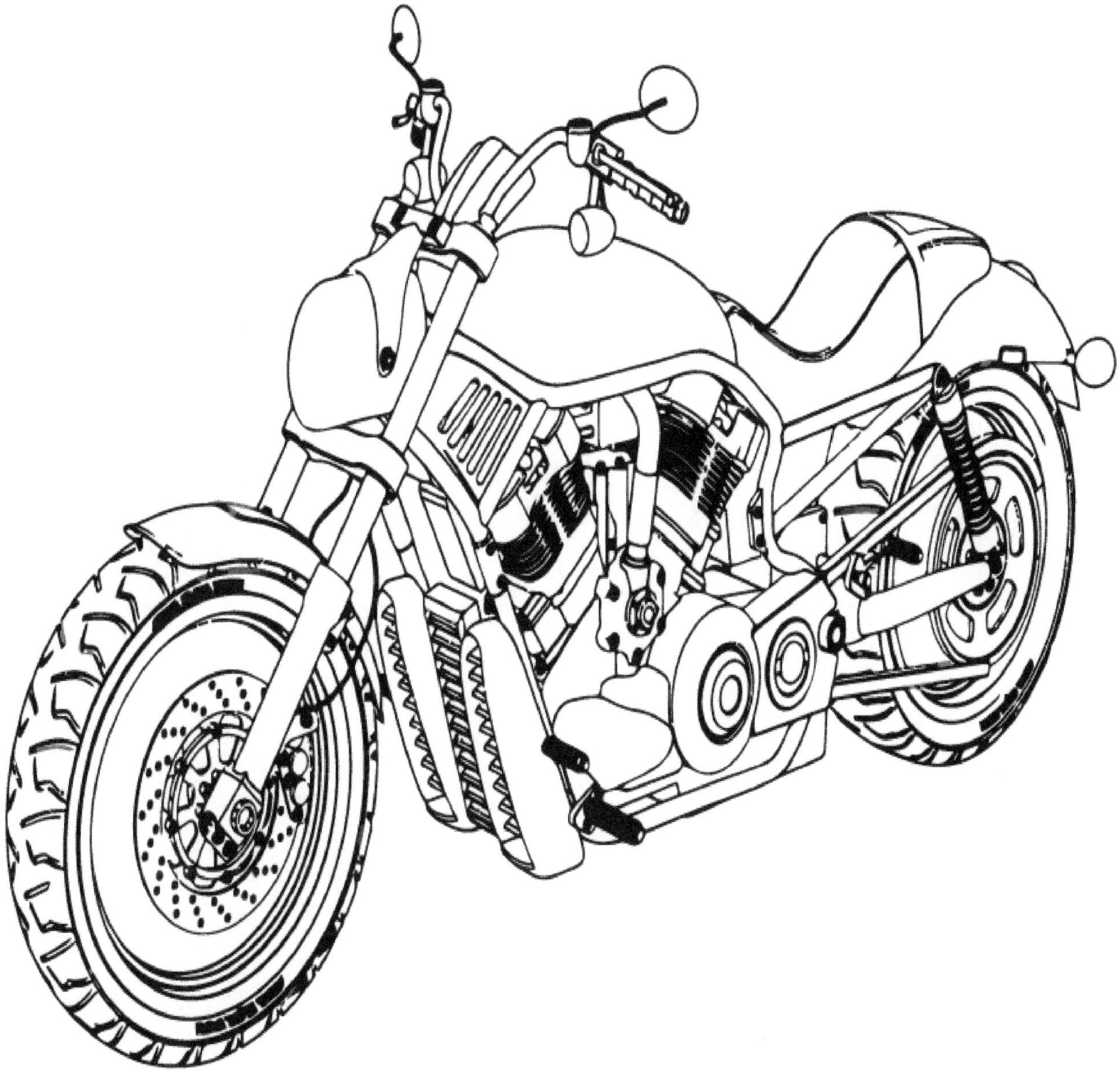

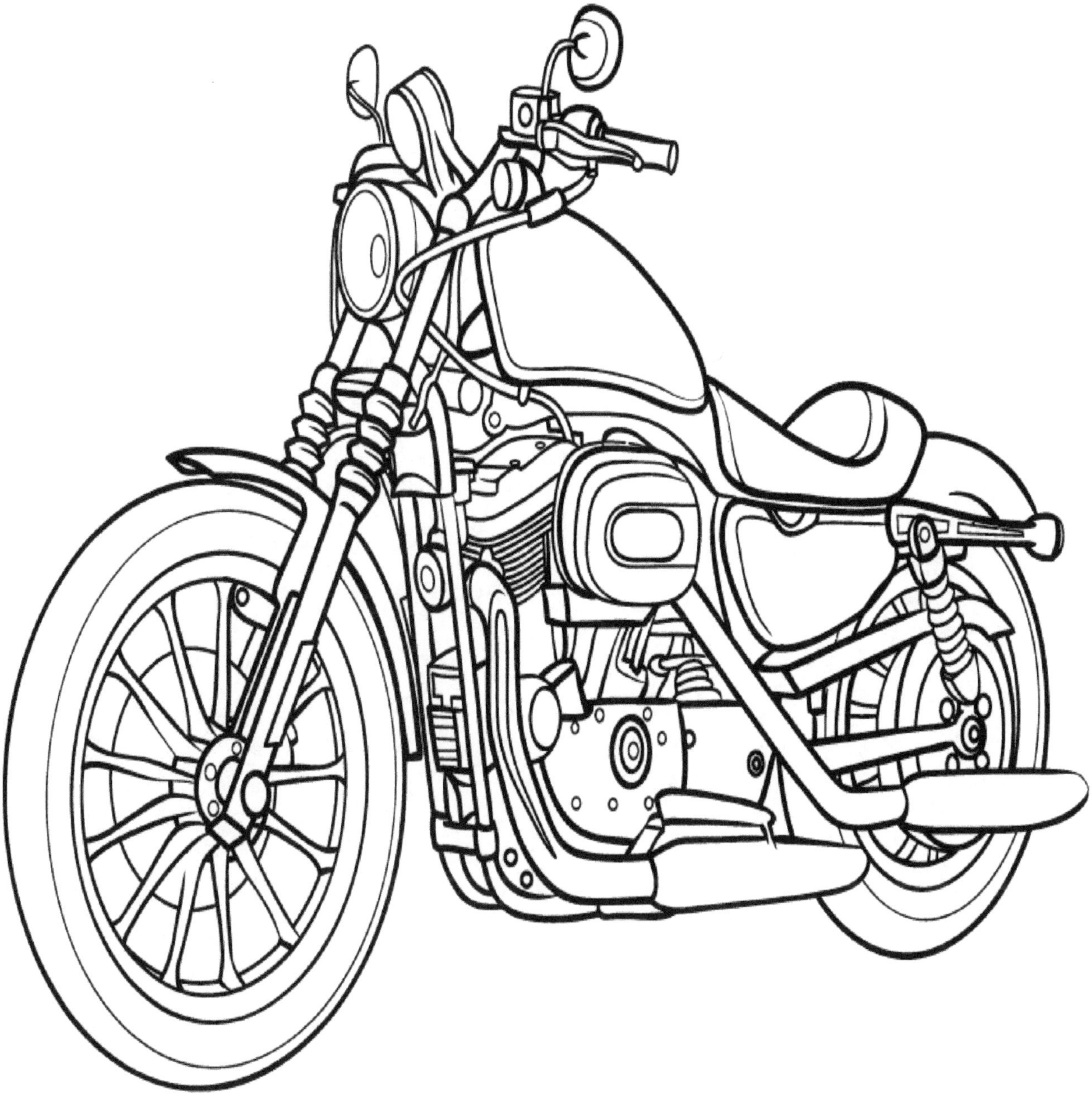

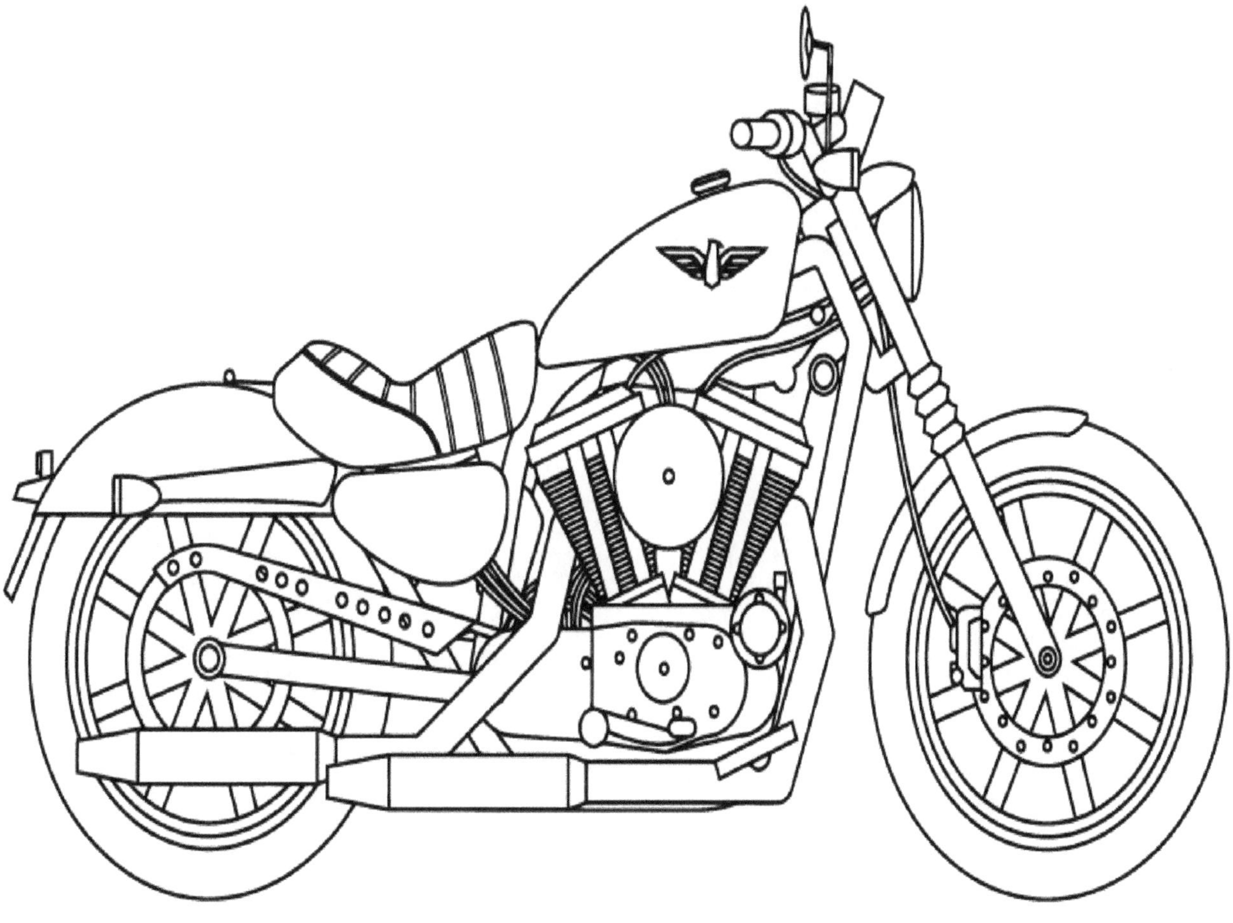

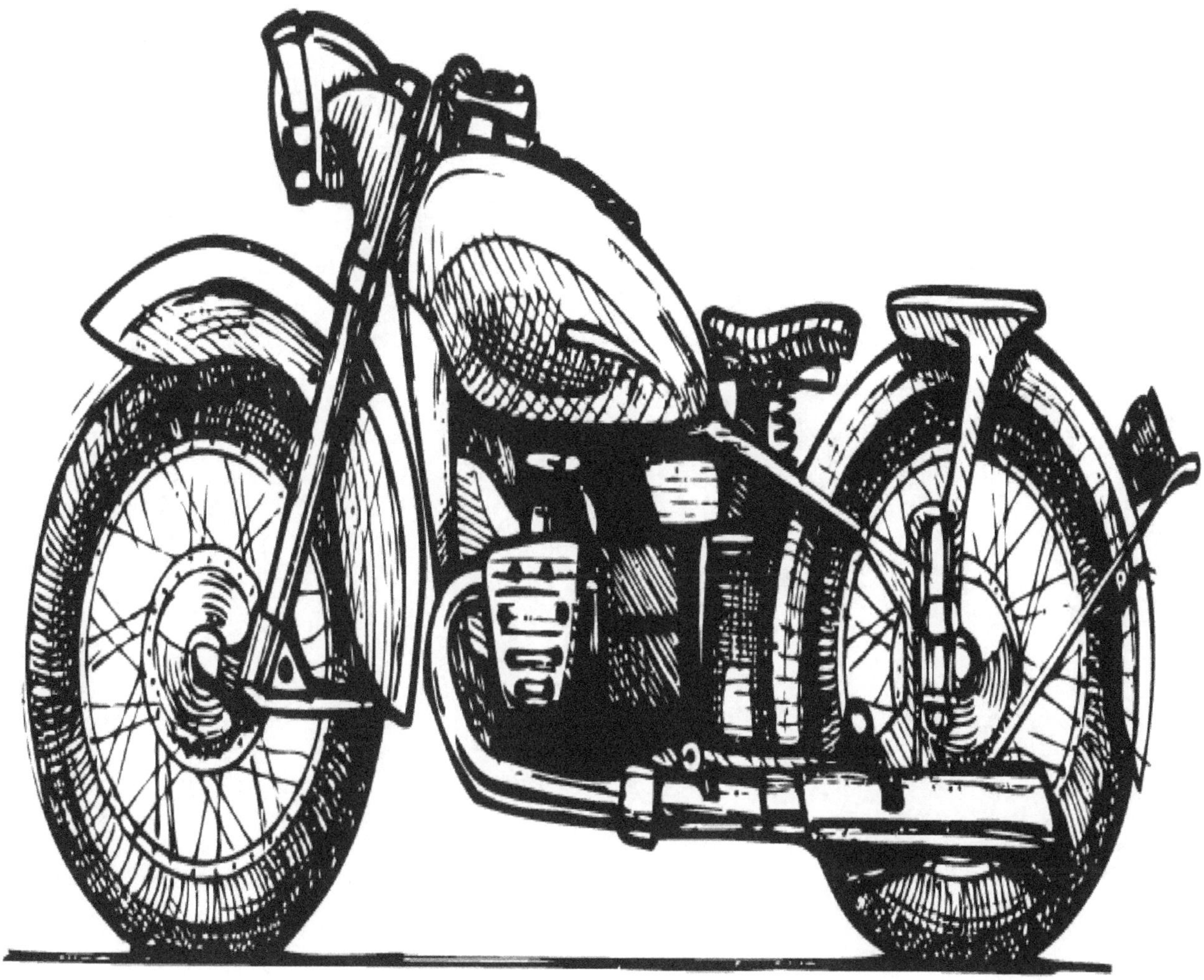

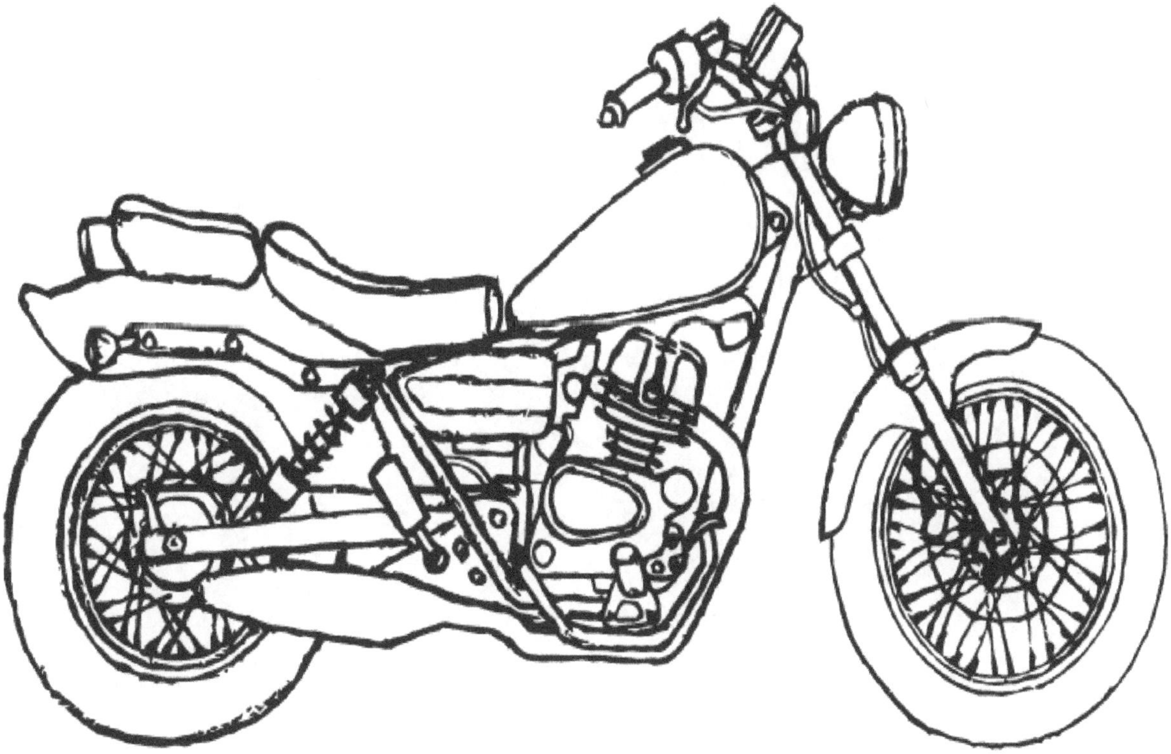

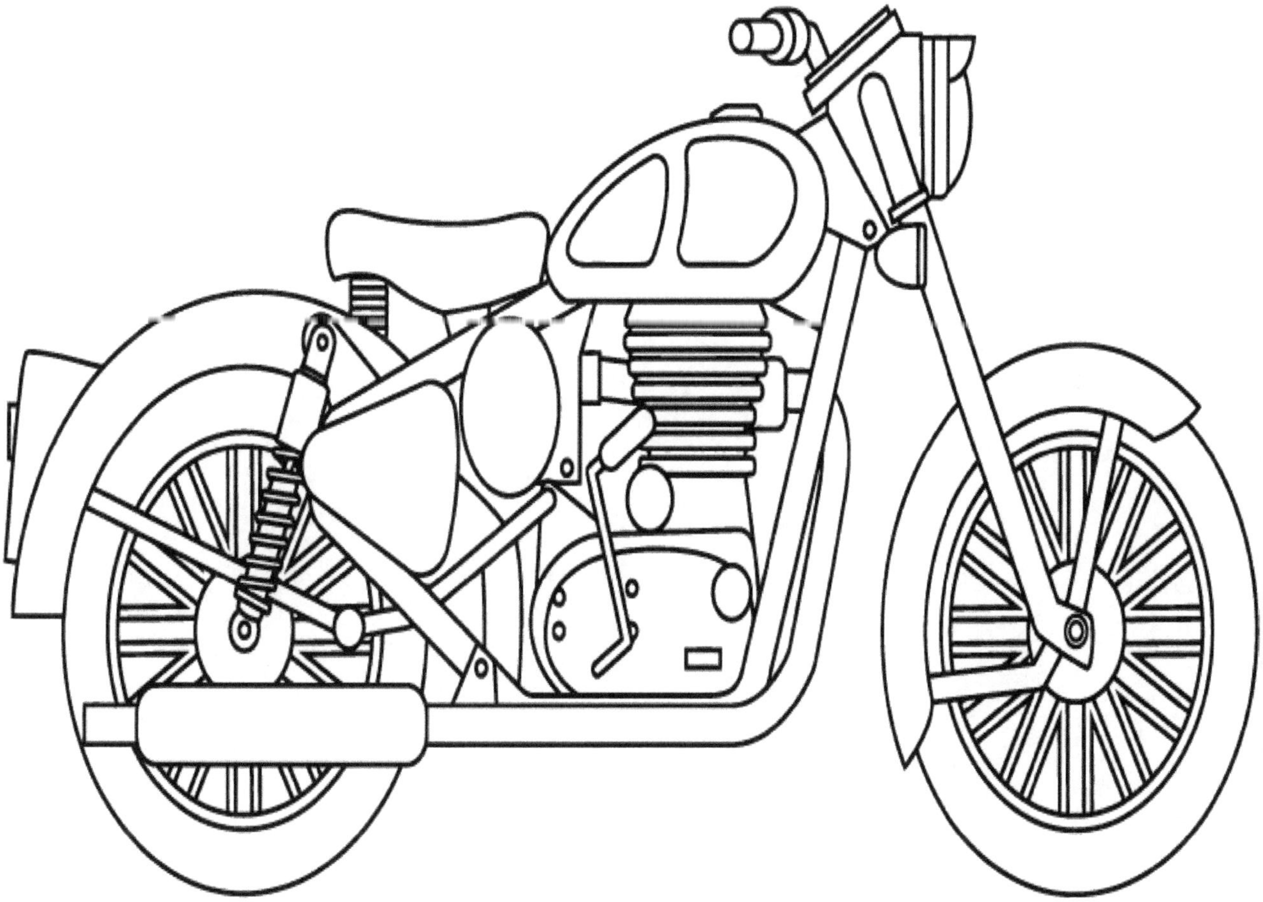

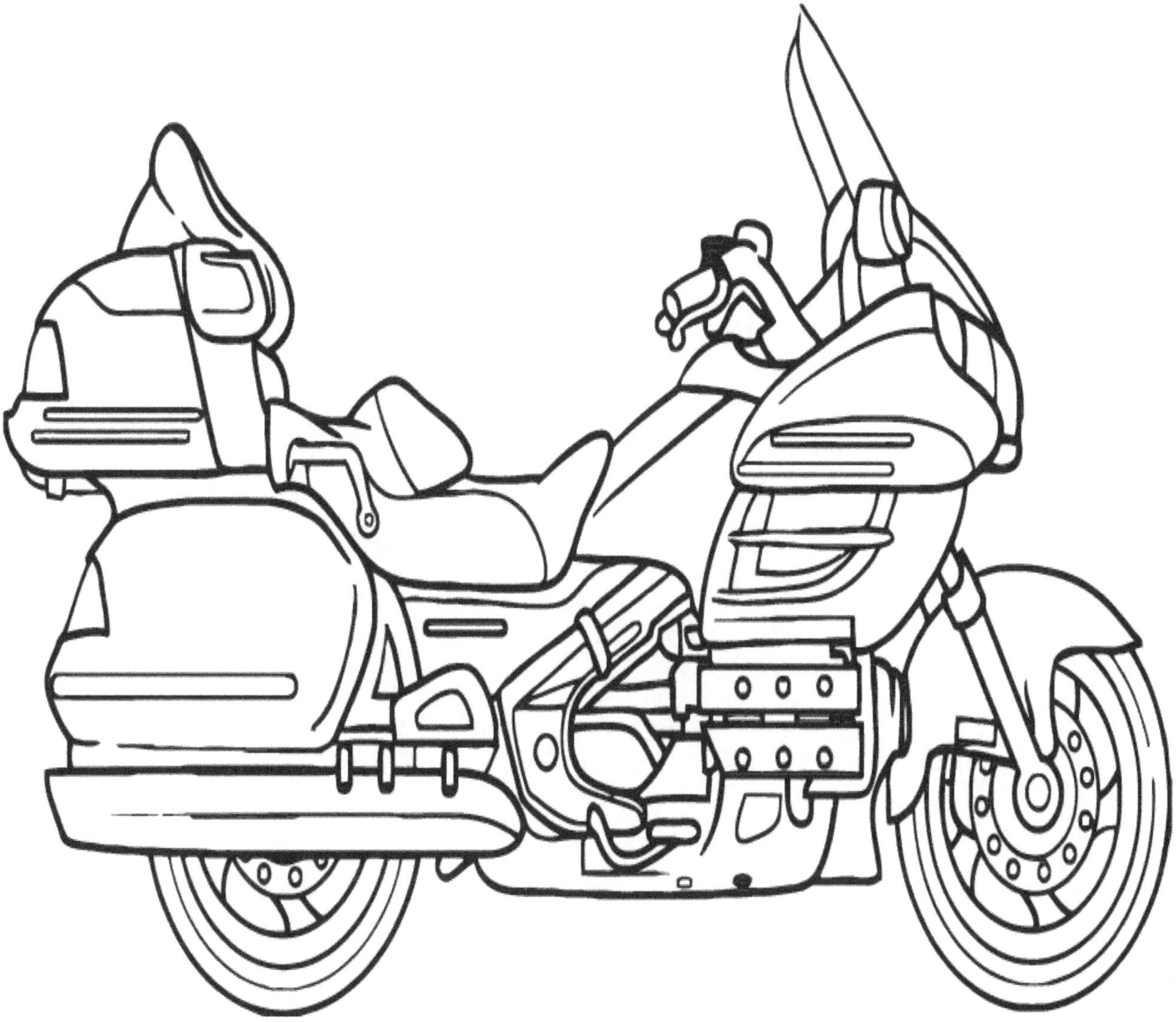

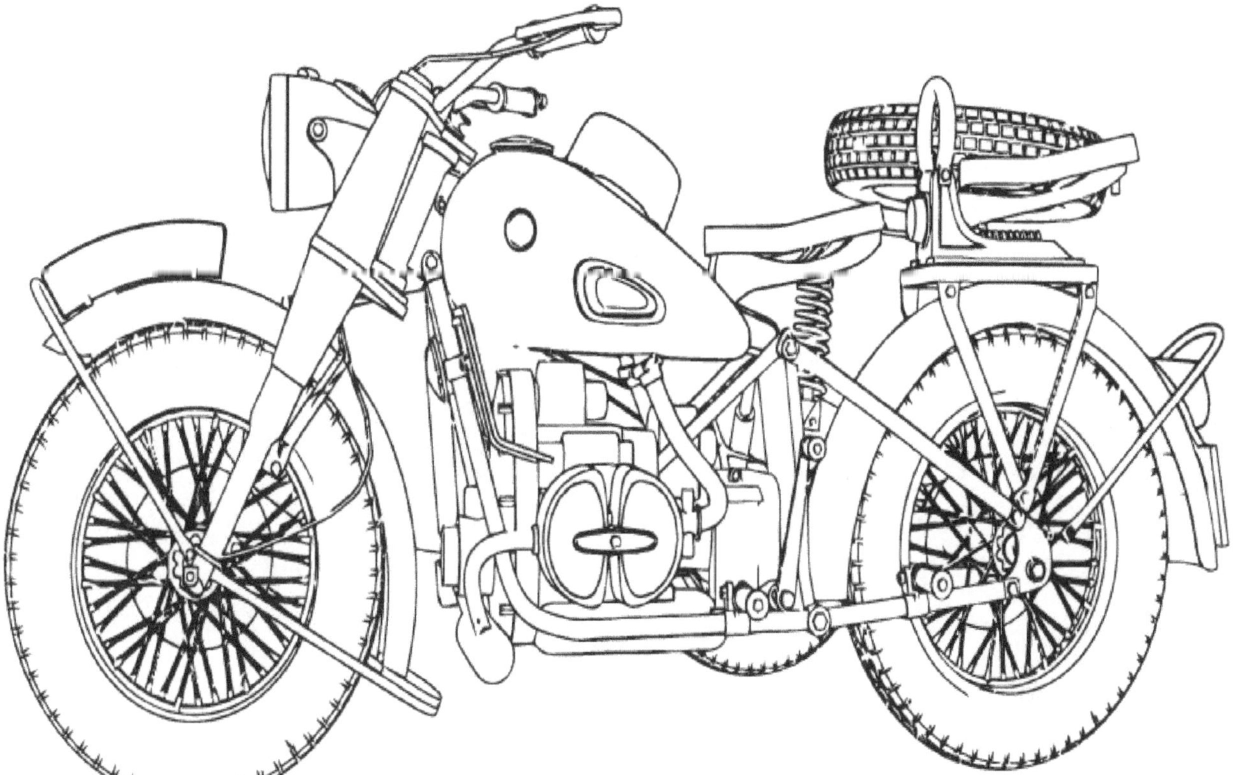

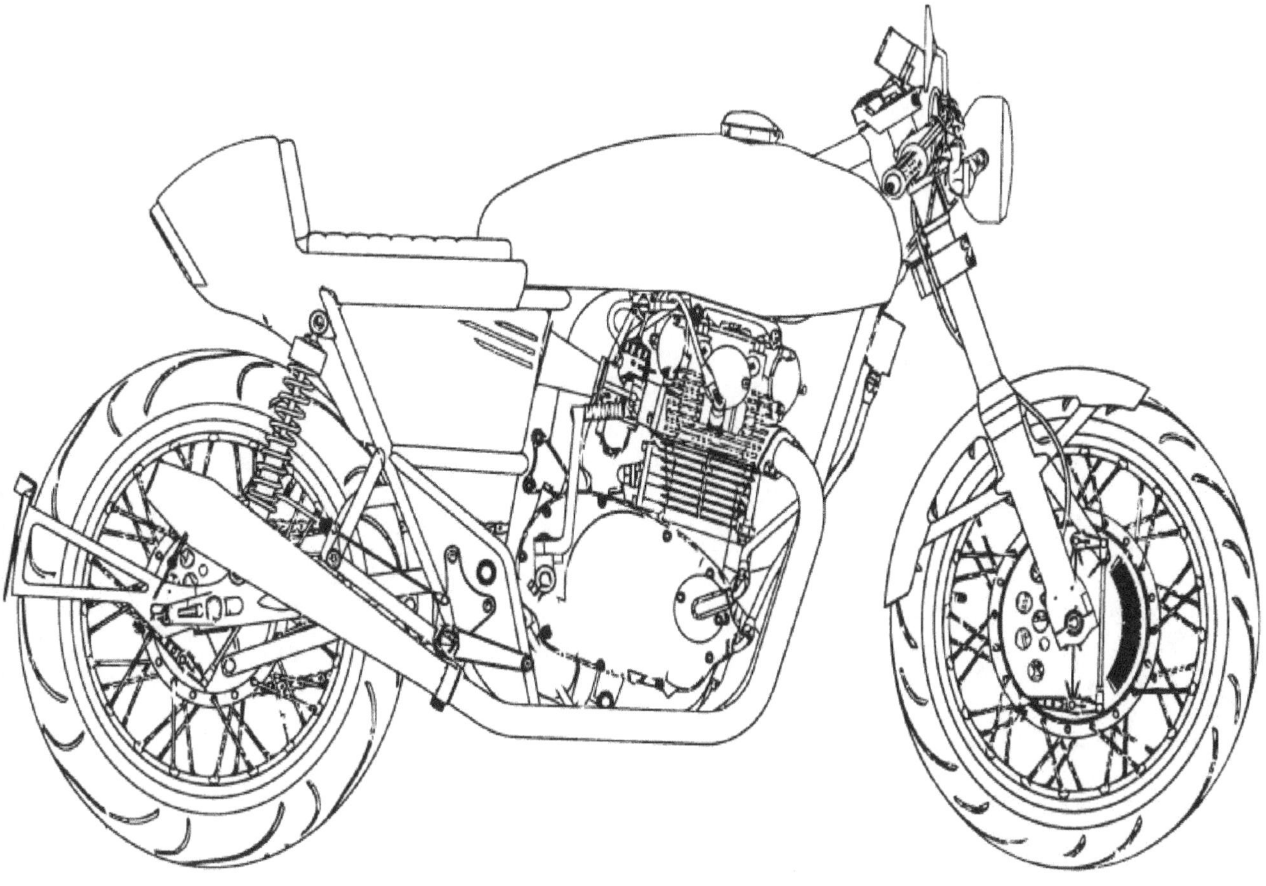

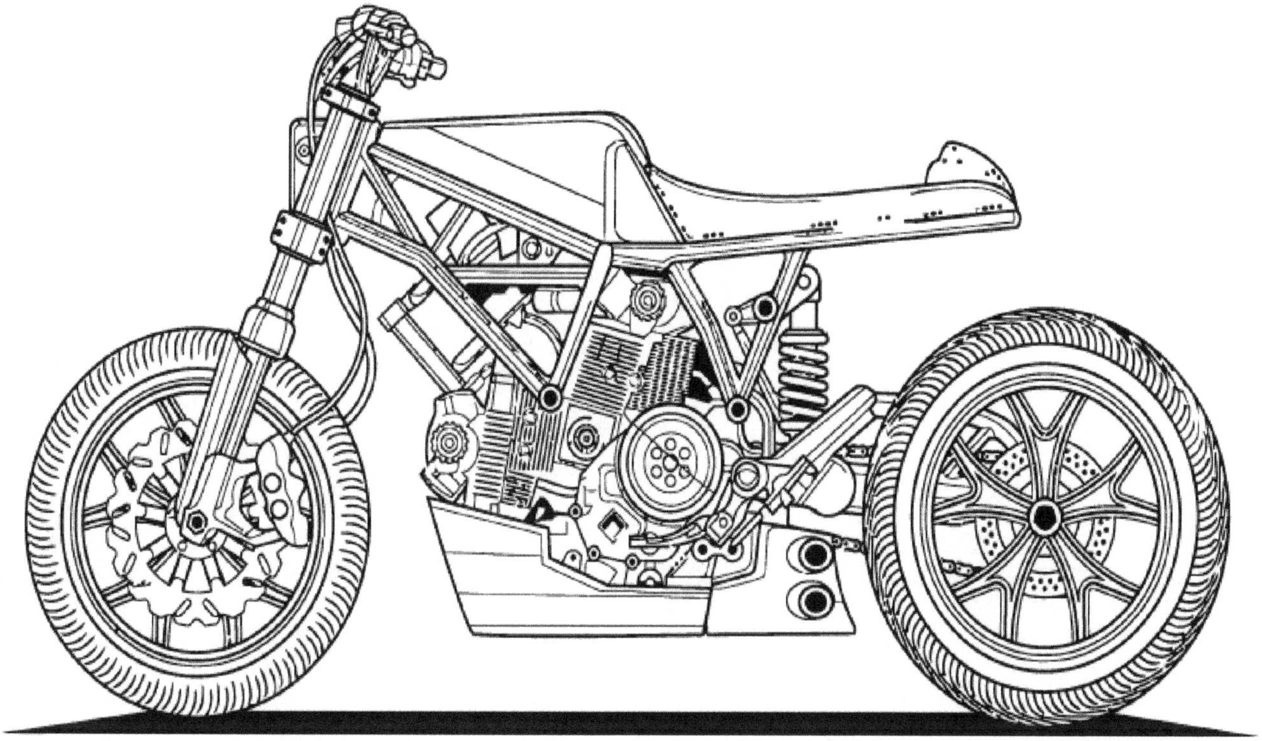

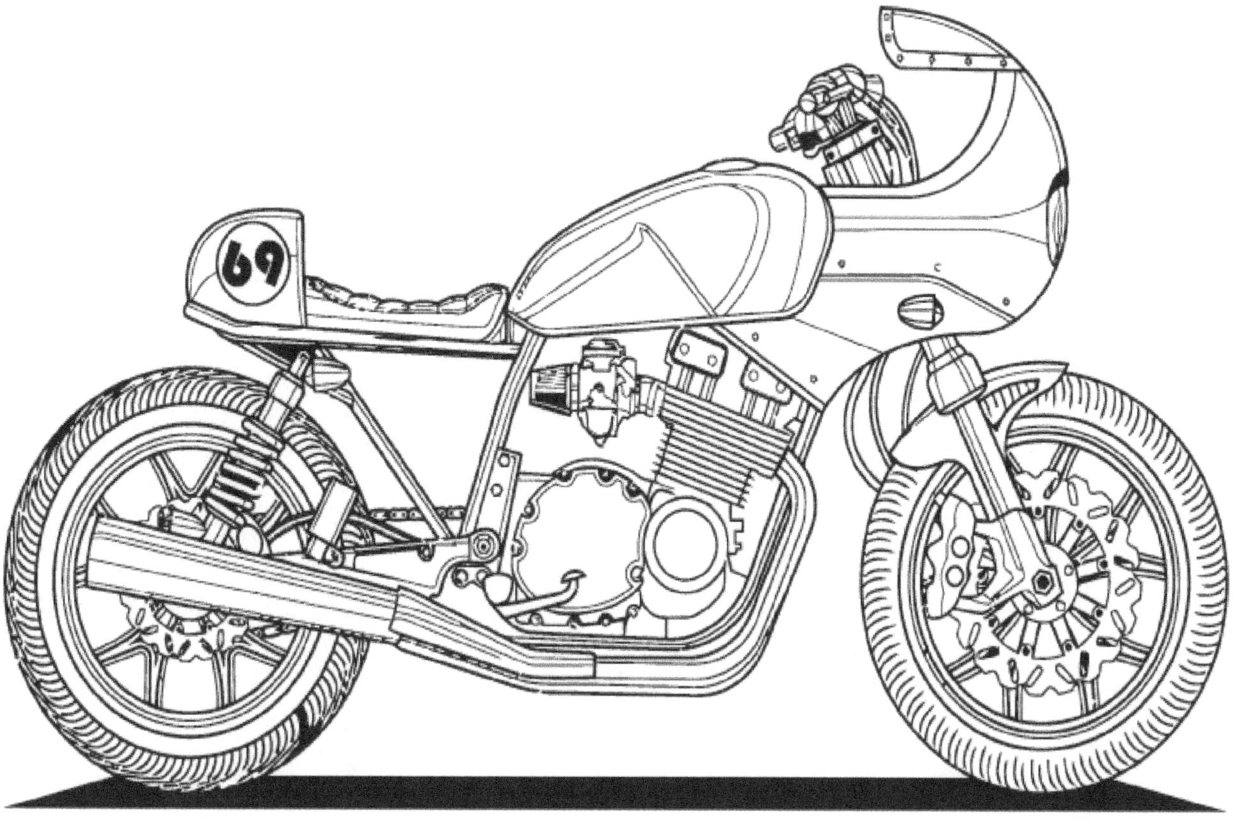
69

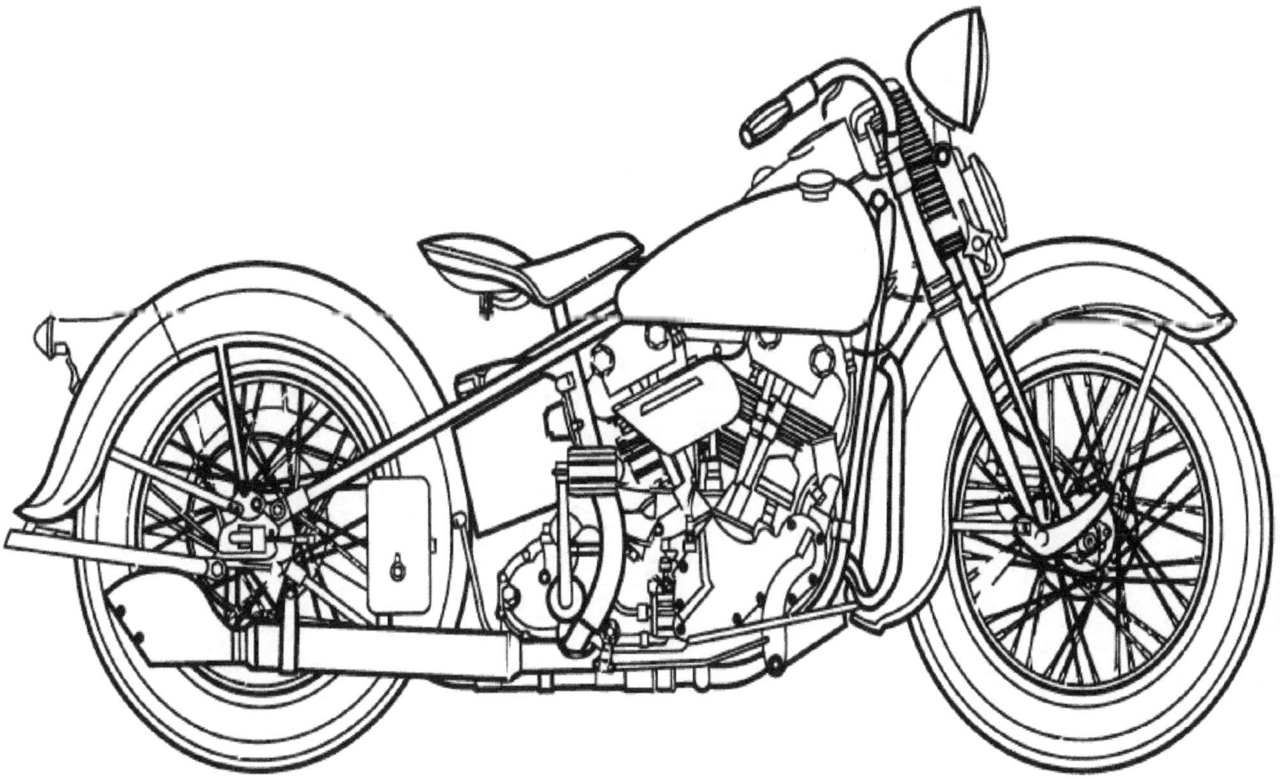

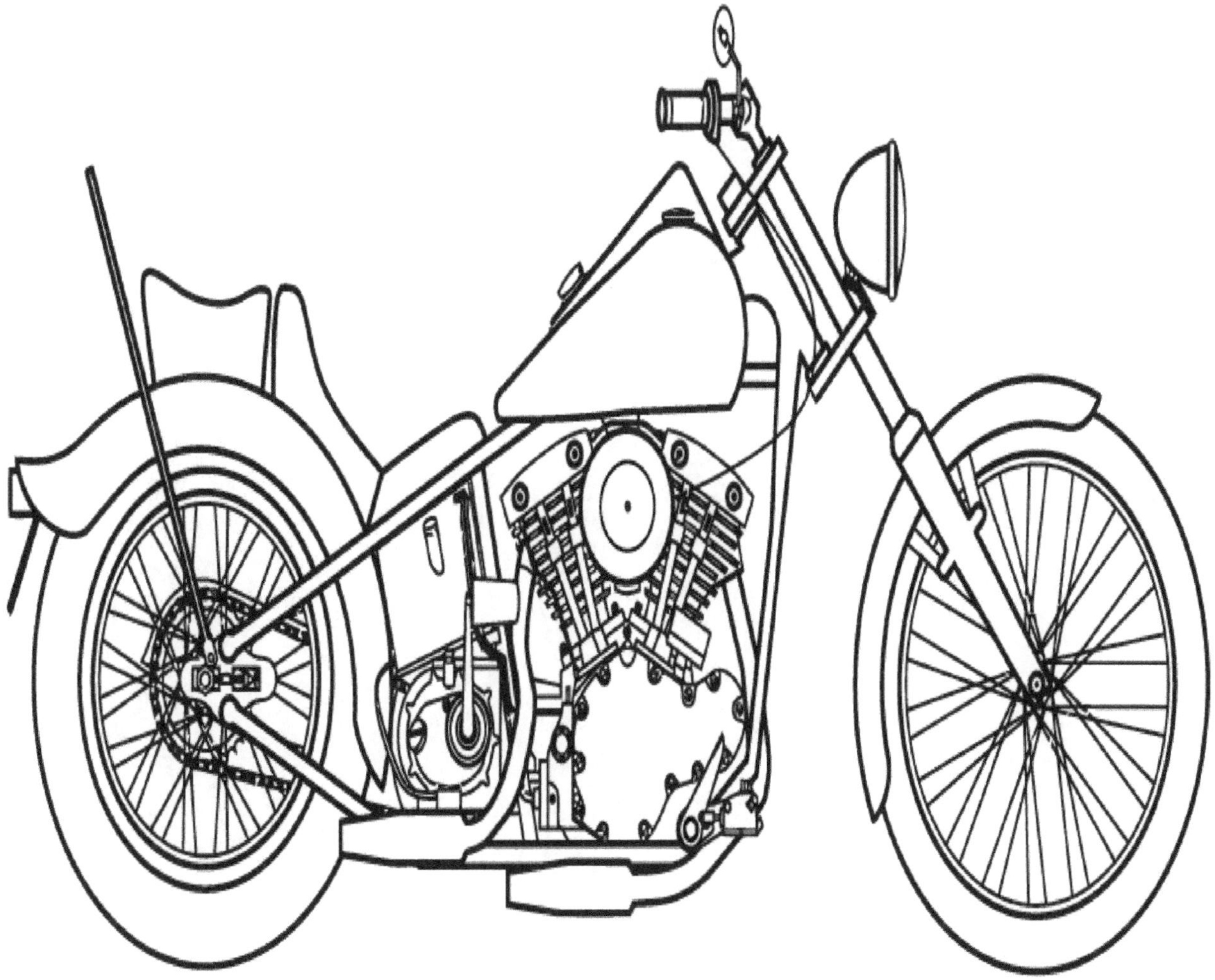

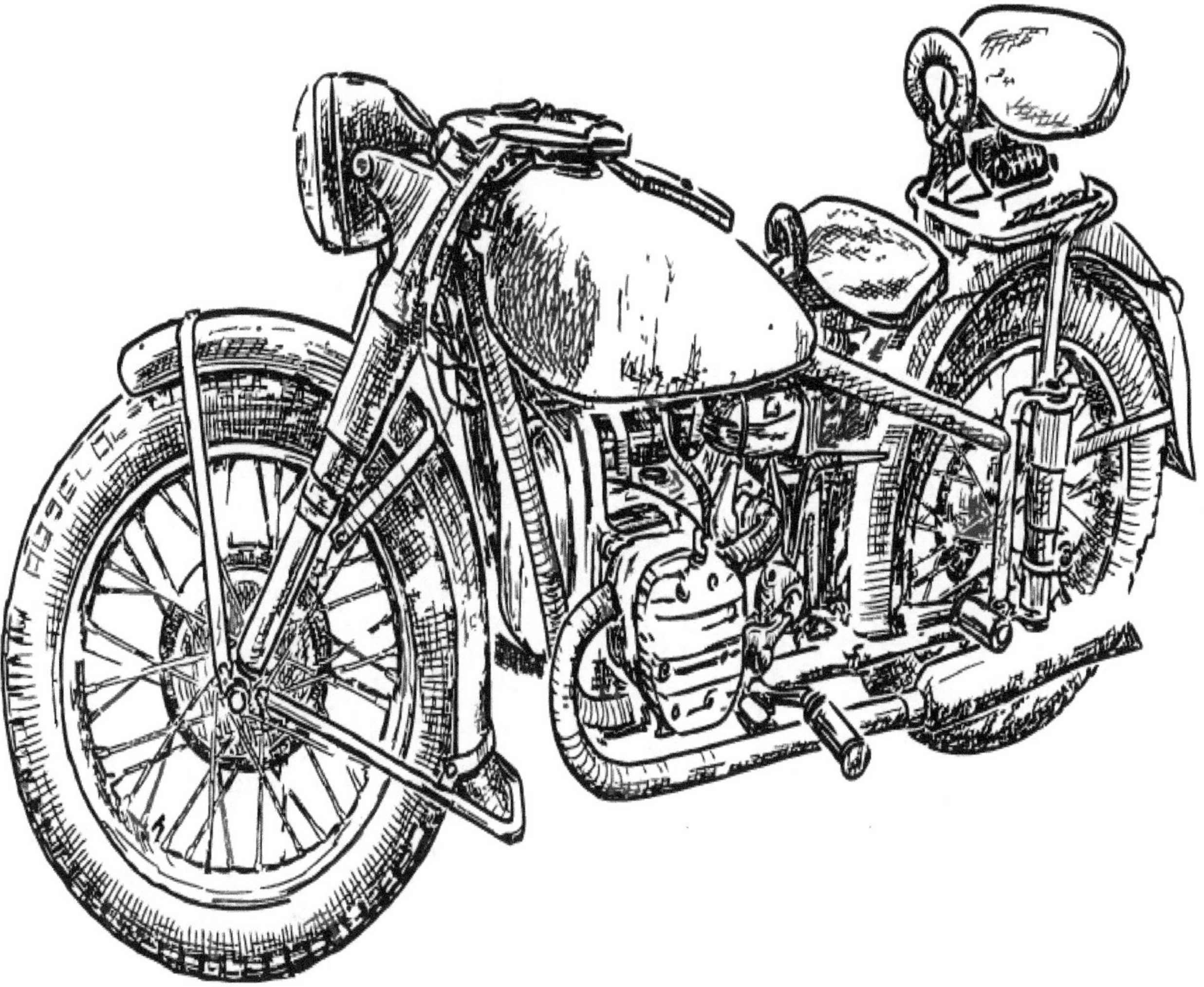

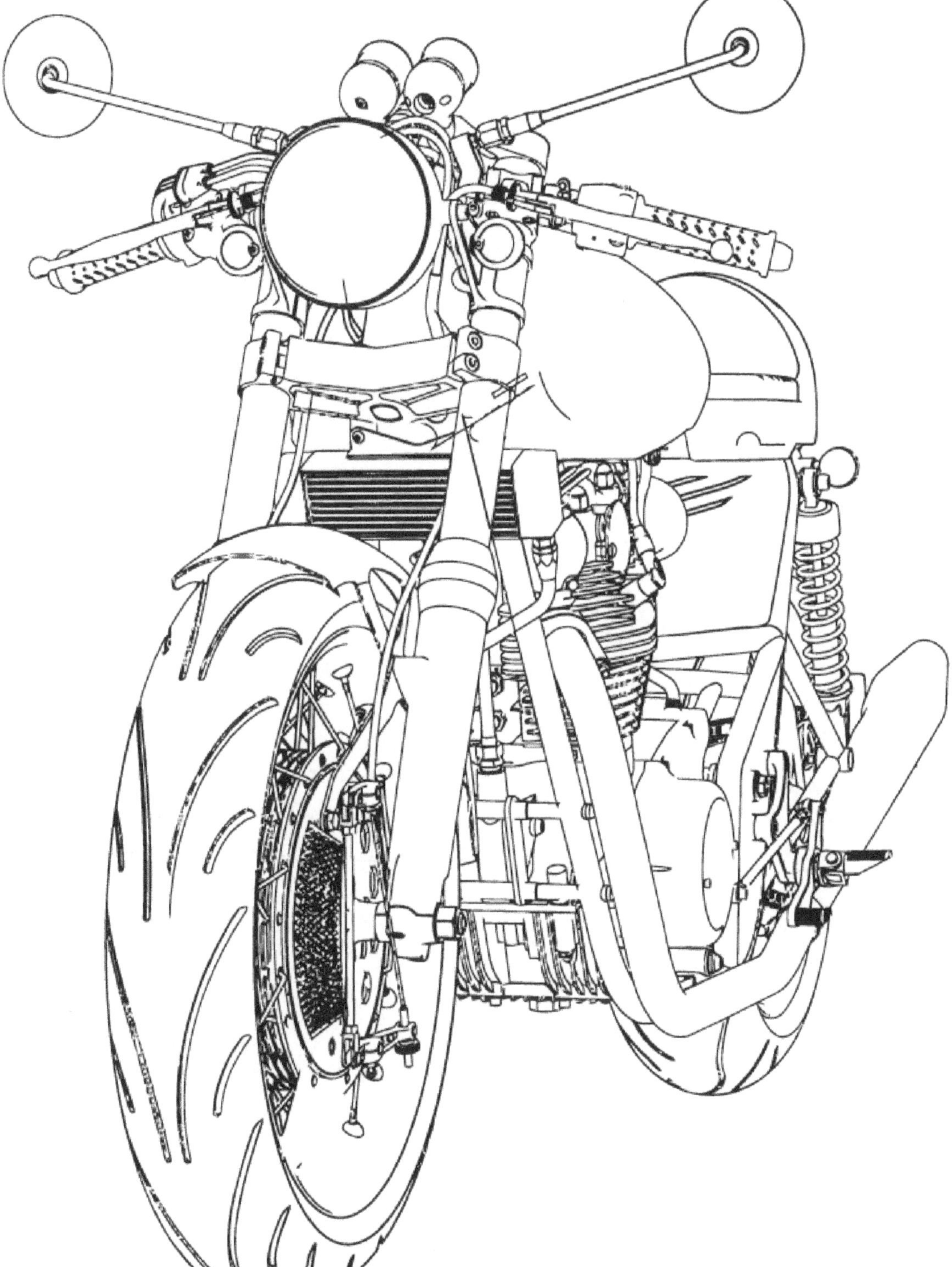

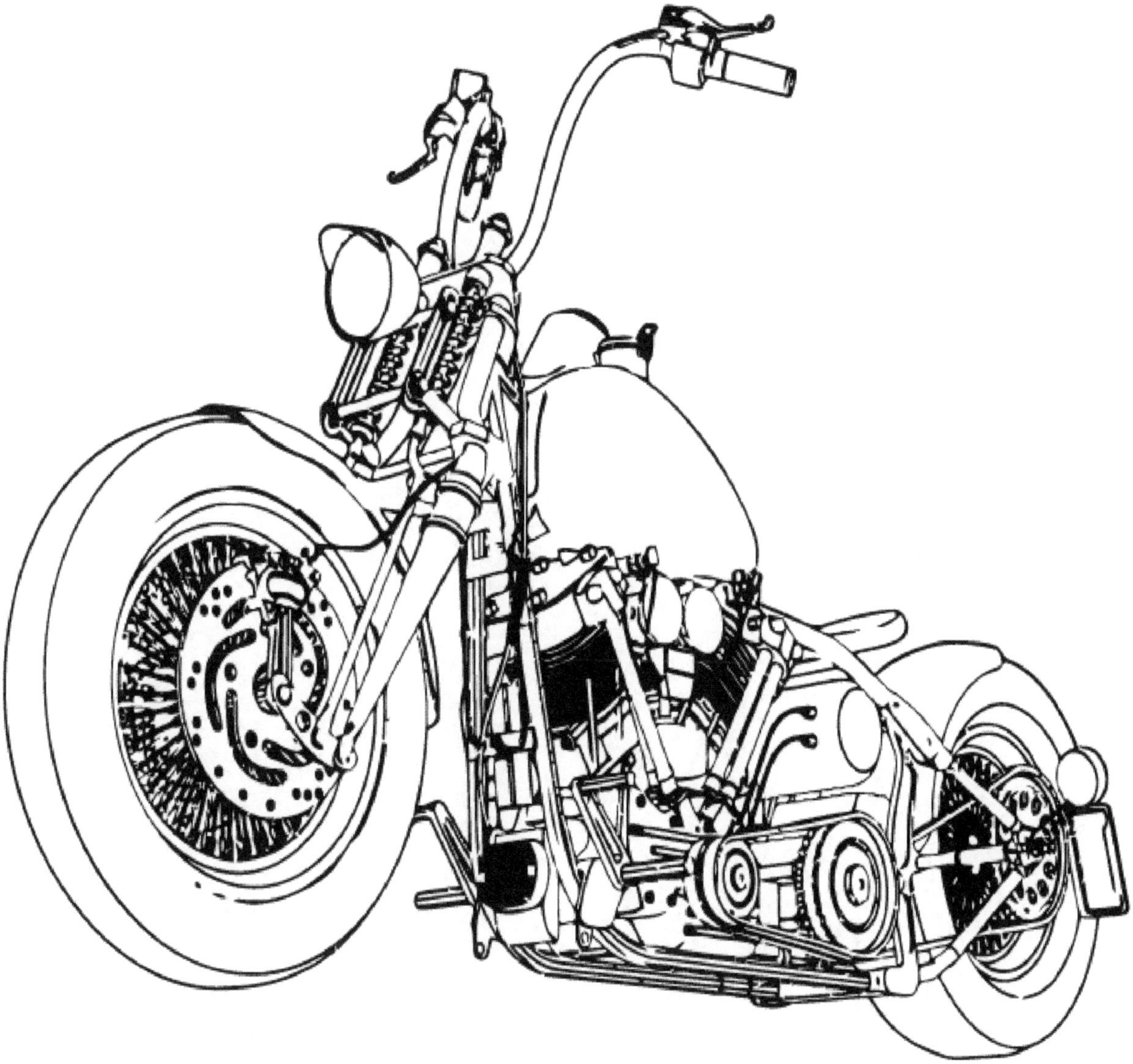

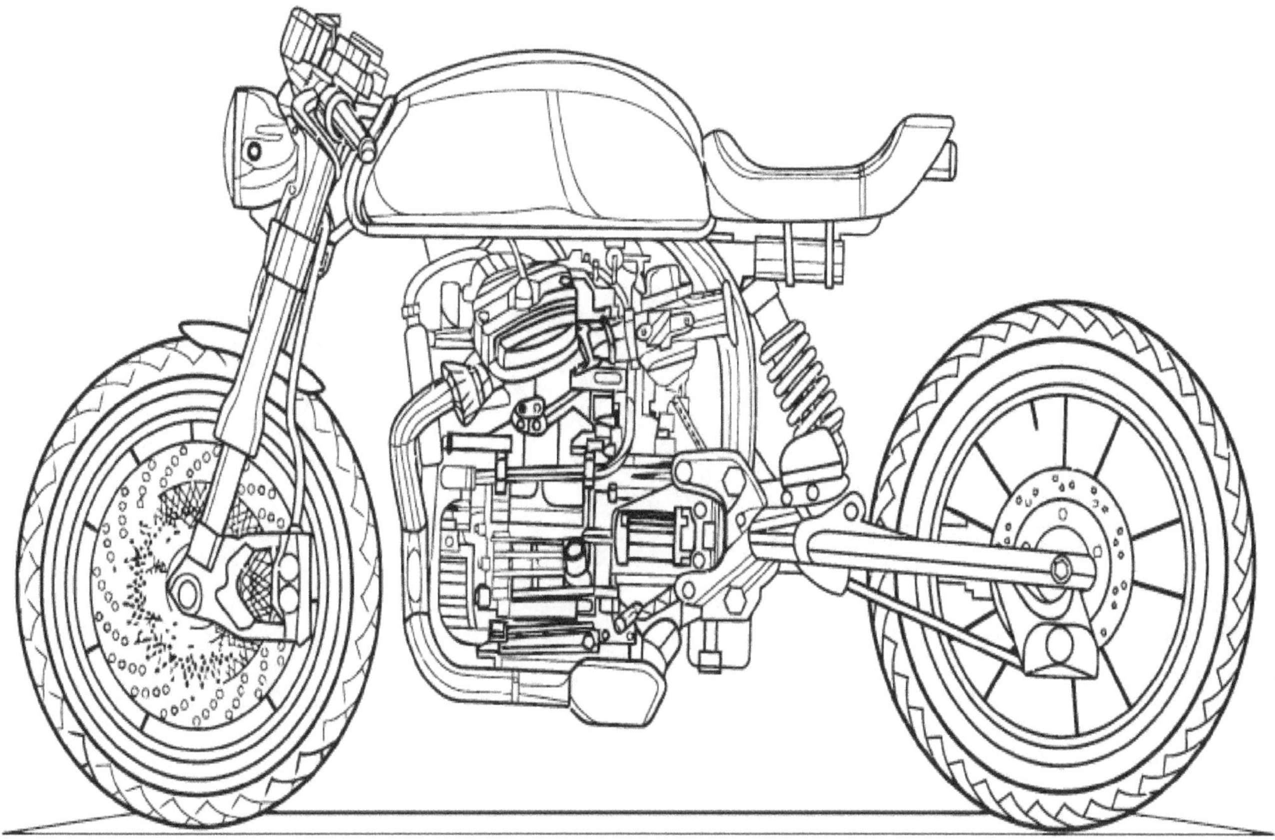

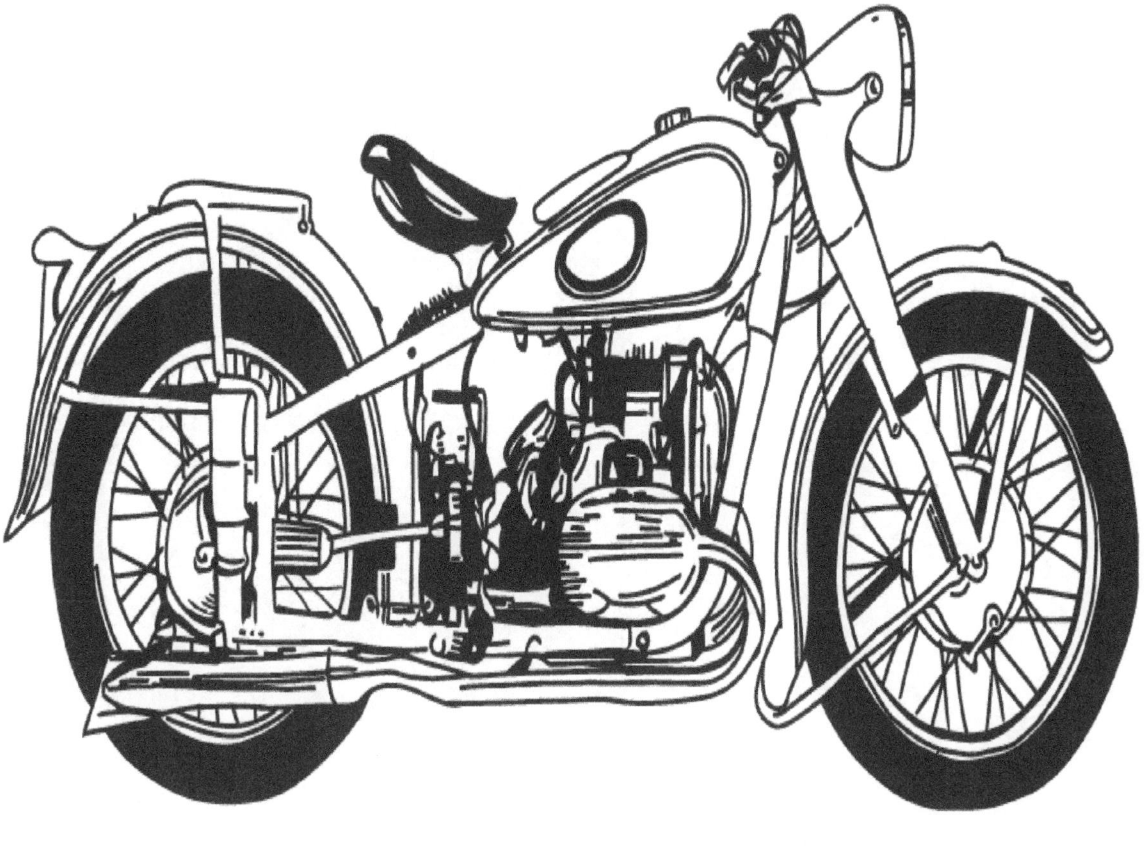

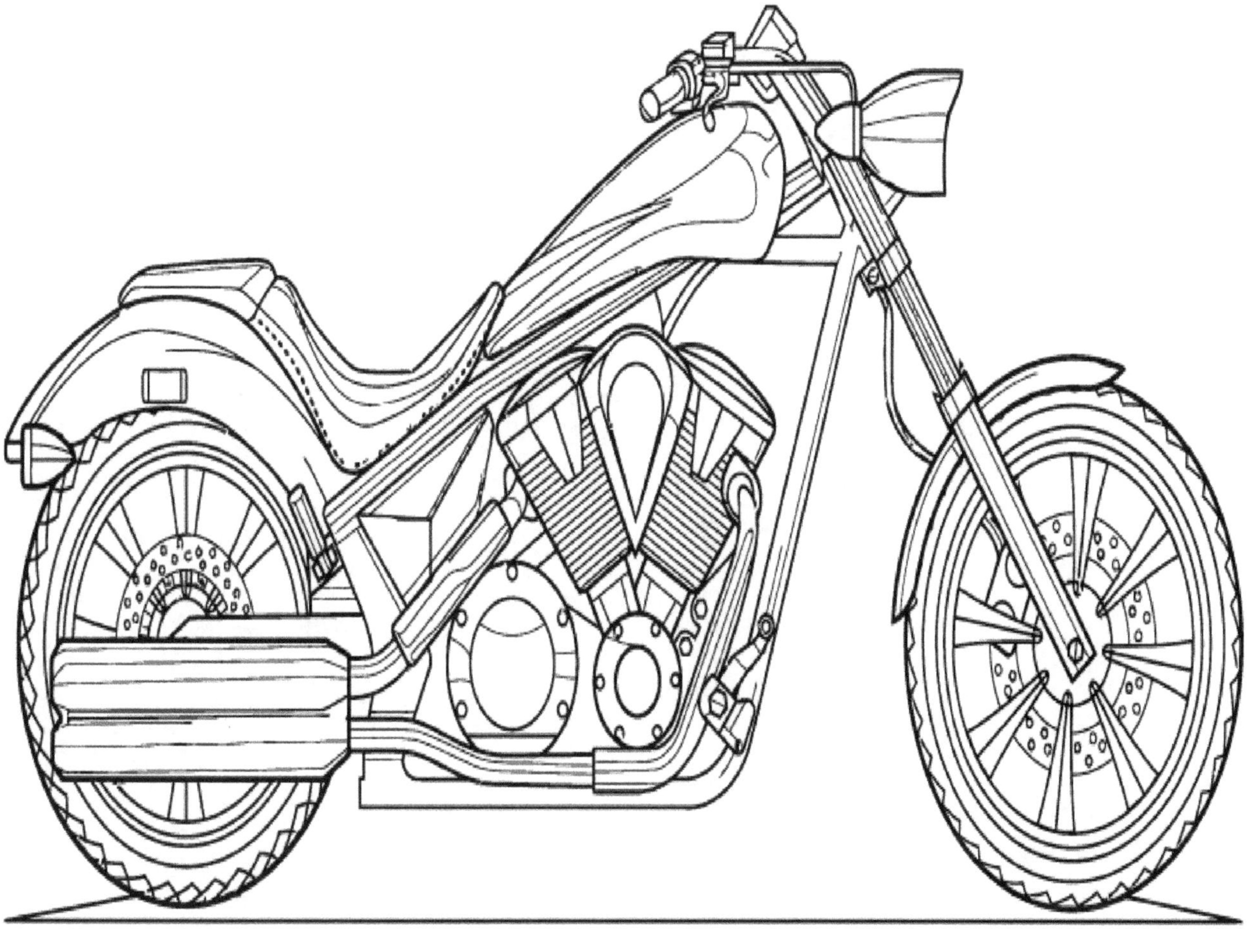

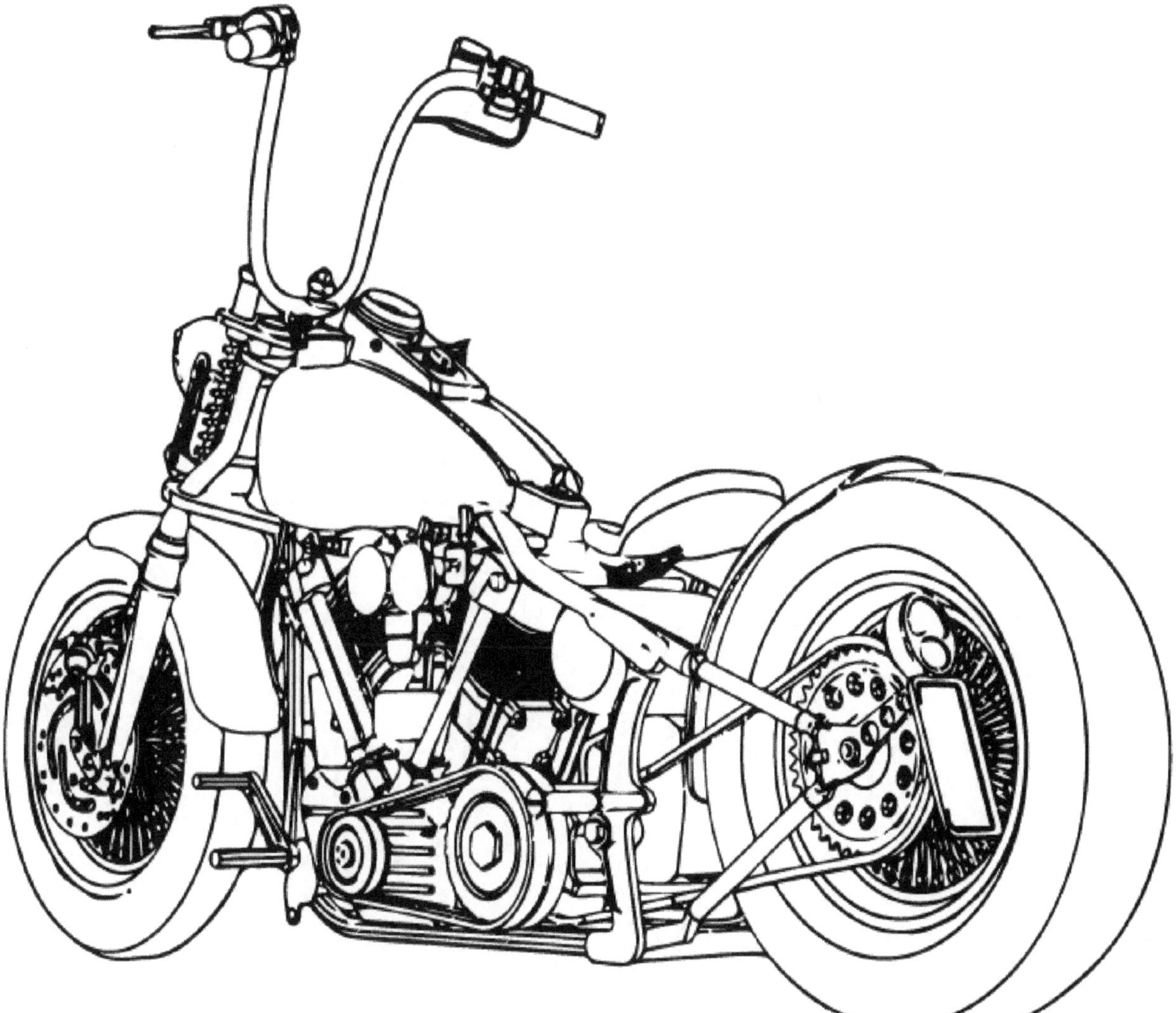

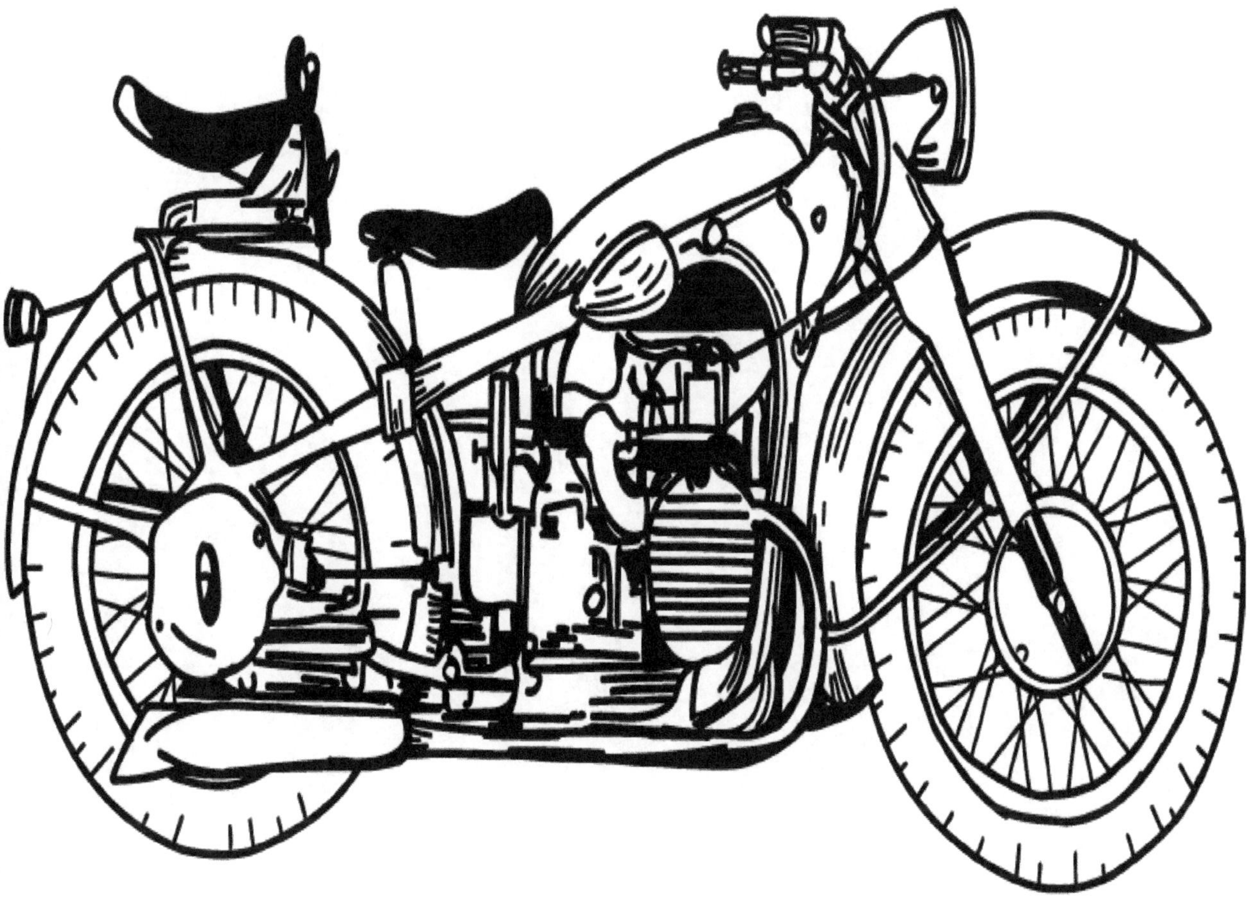

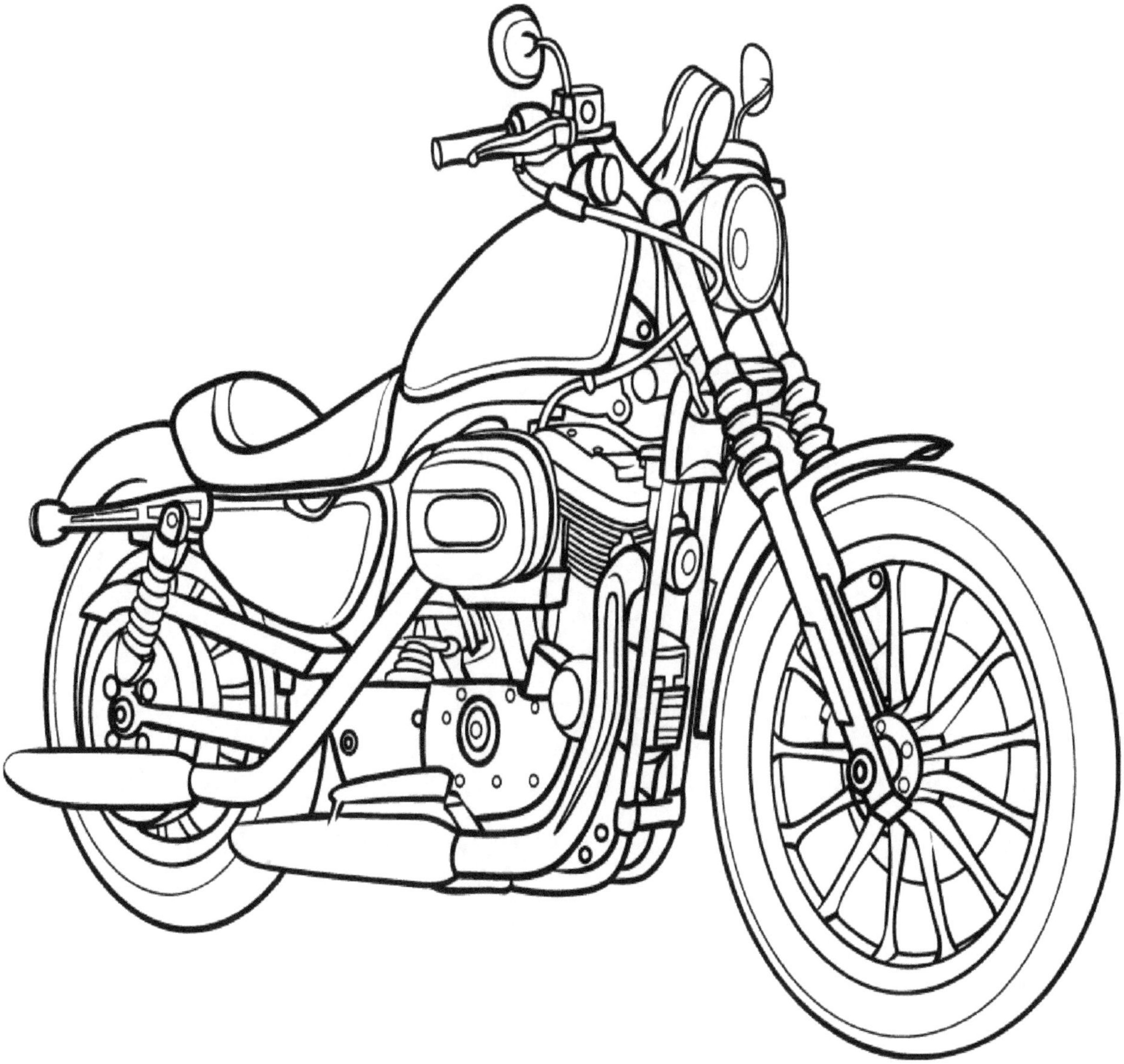

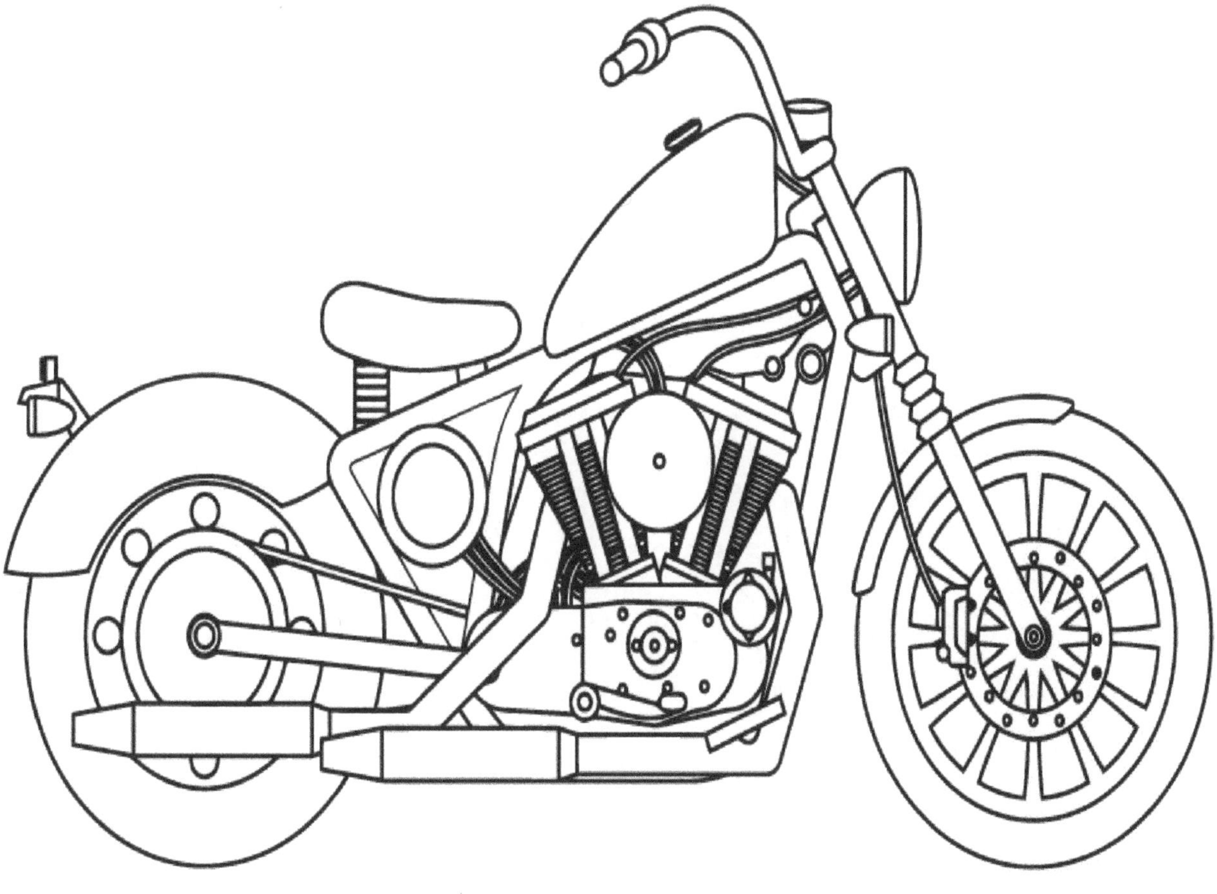

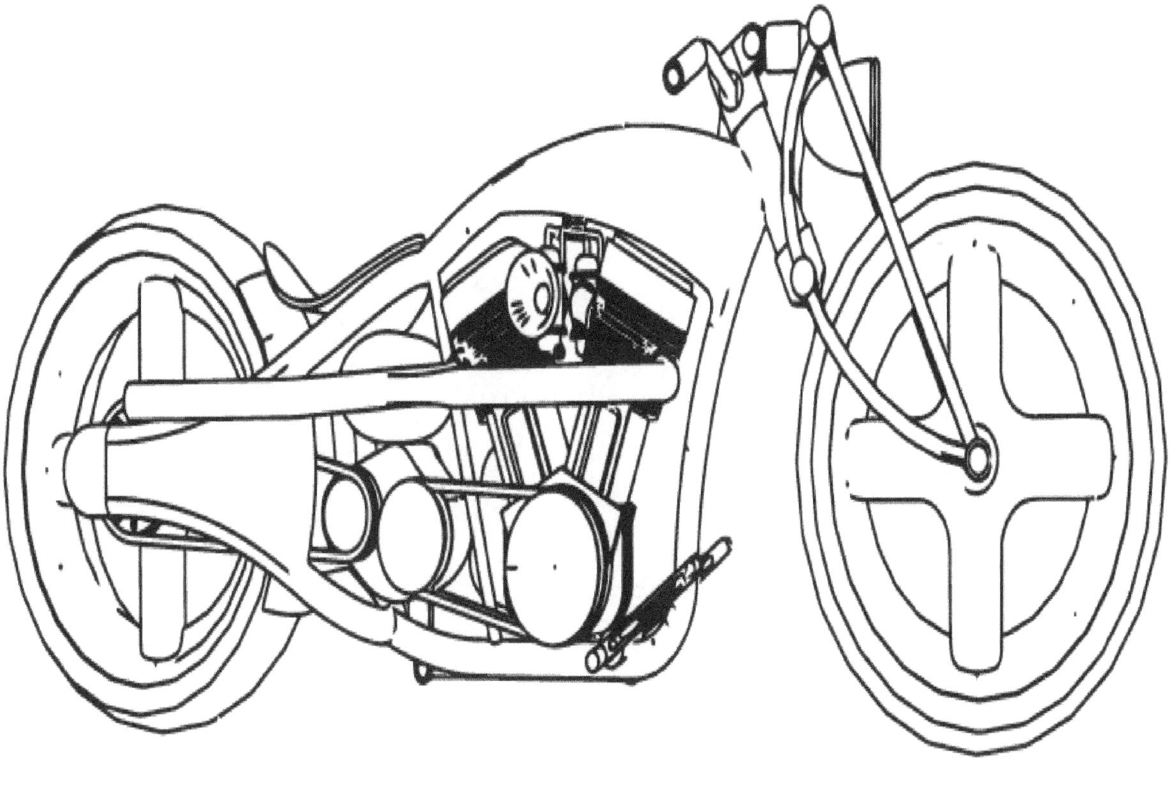

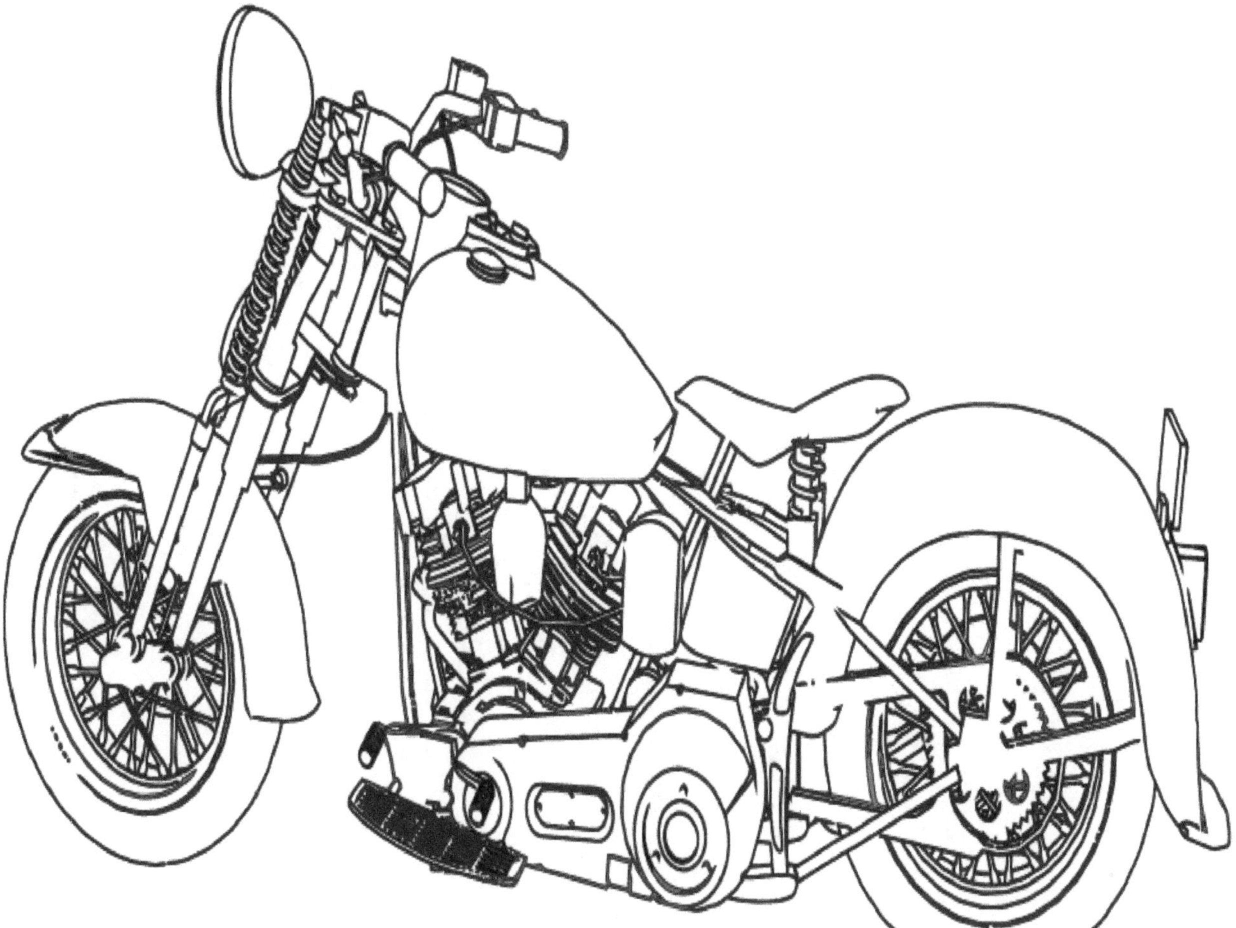

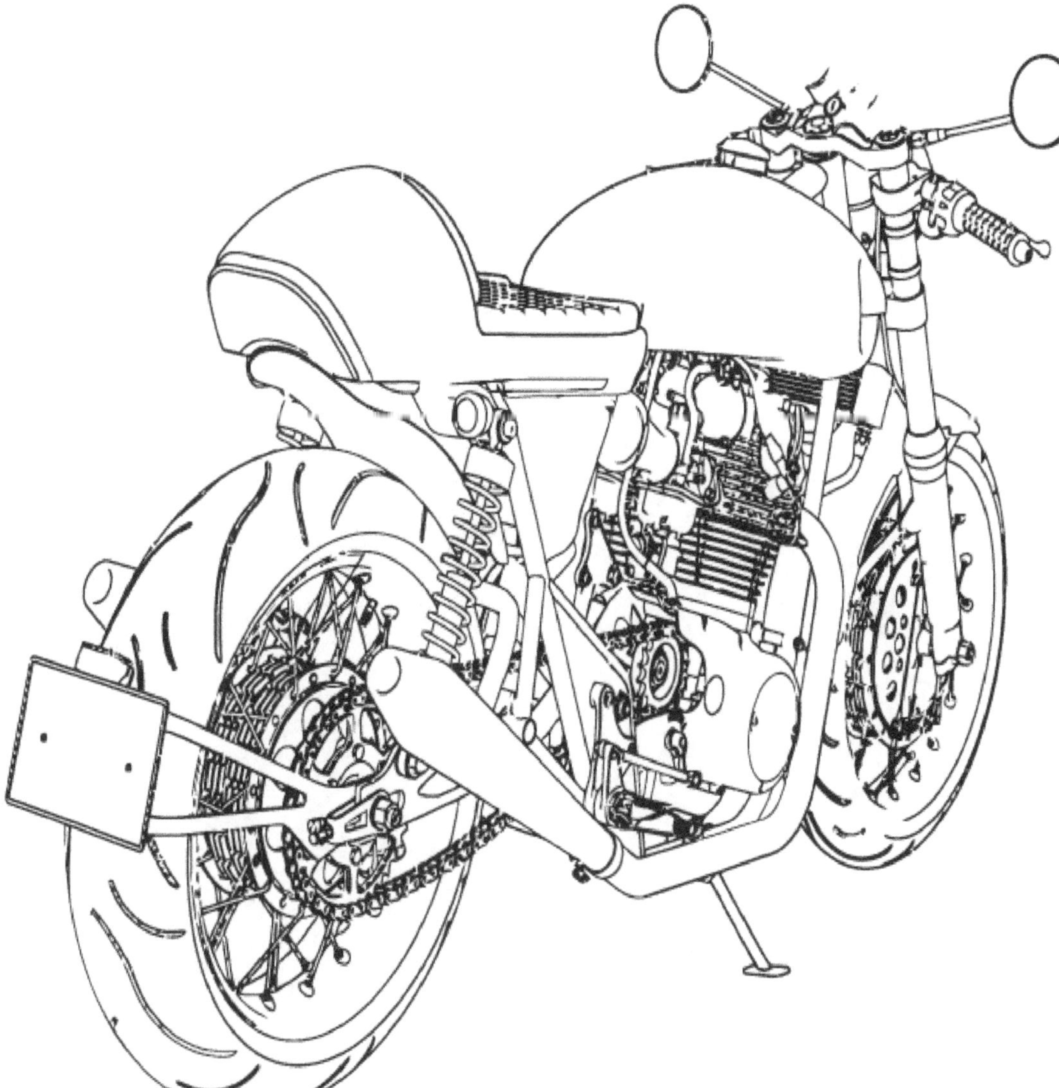

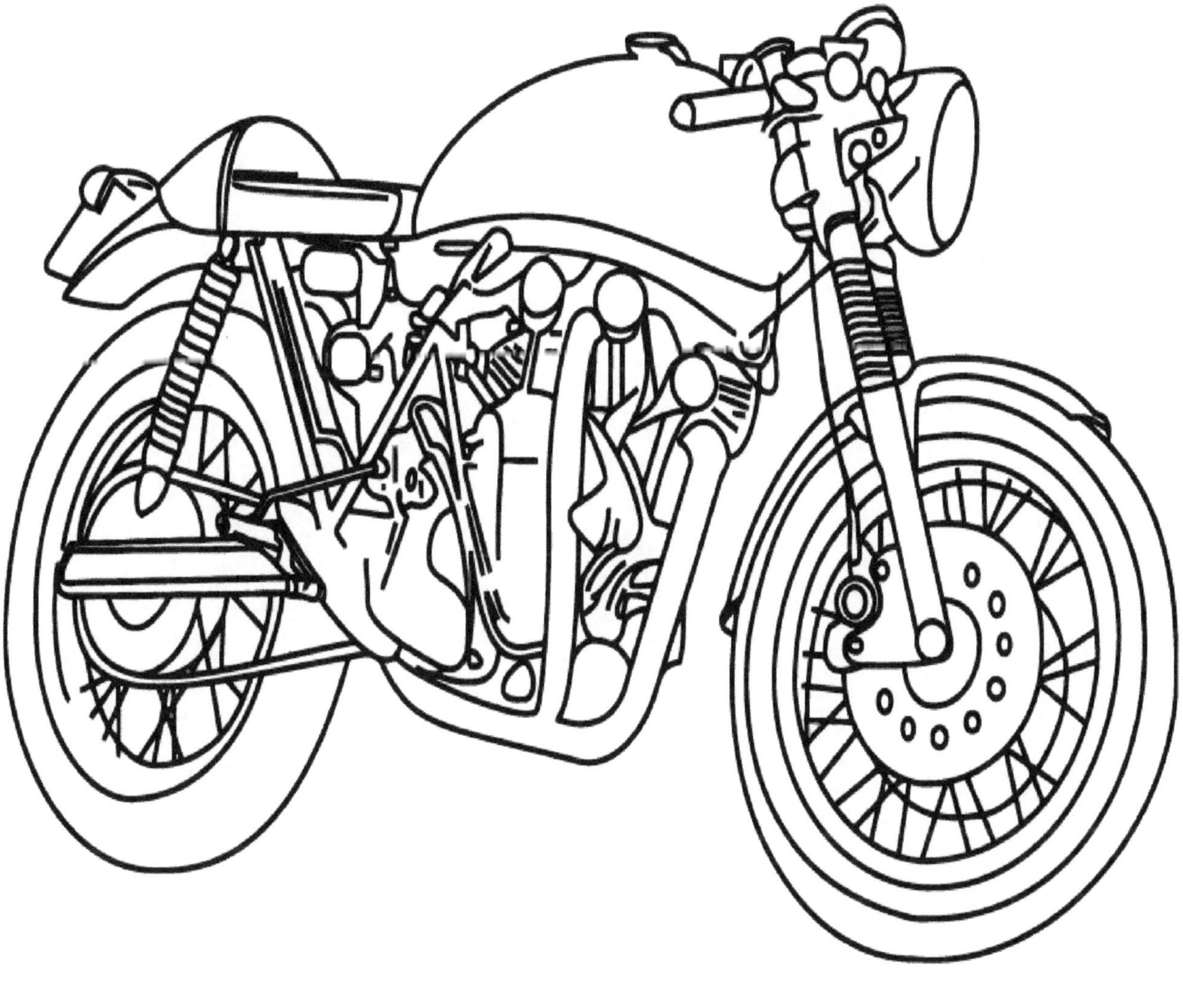

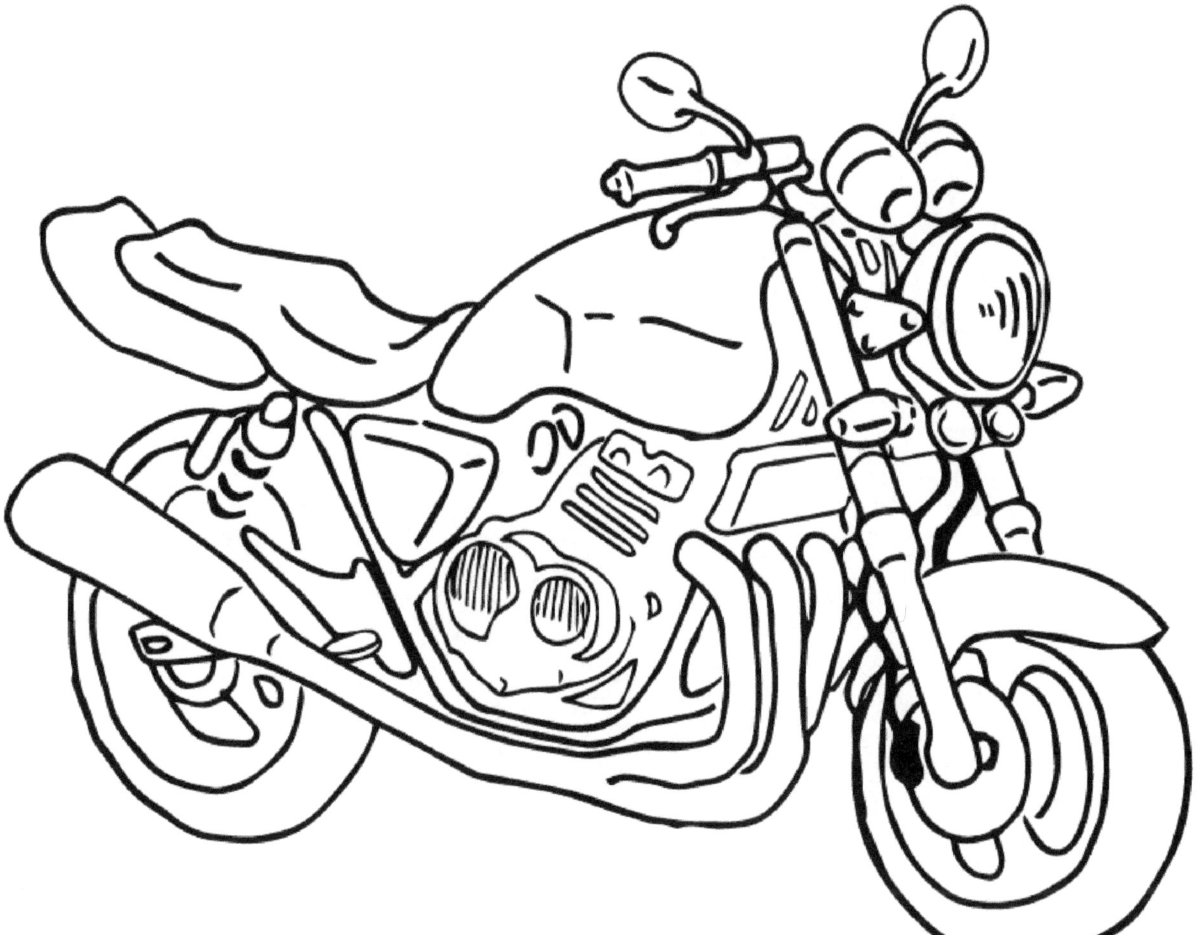

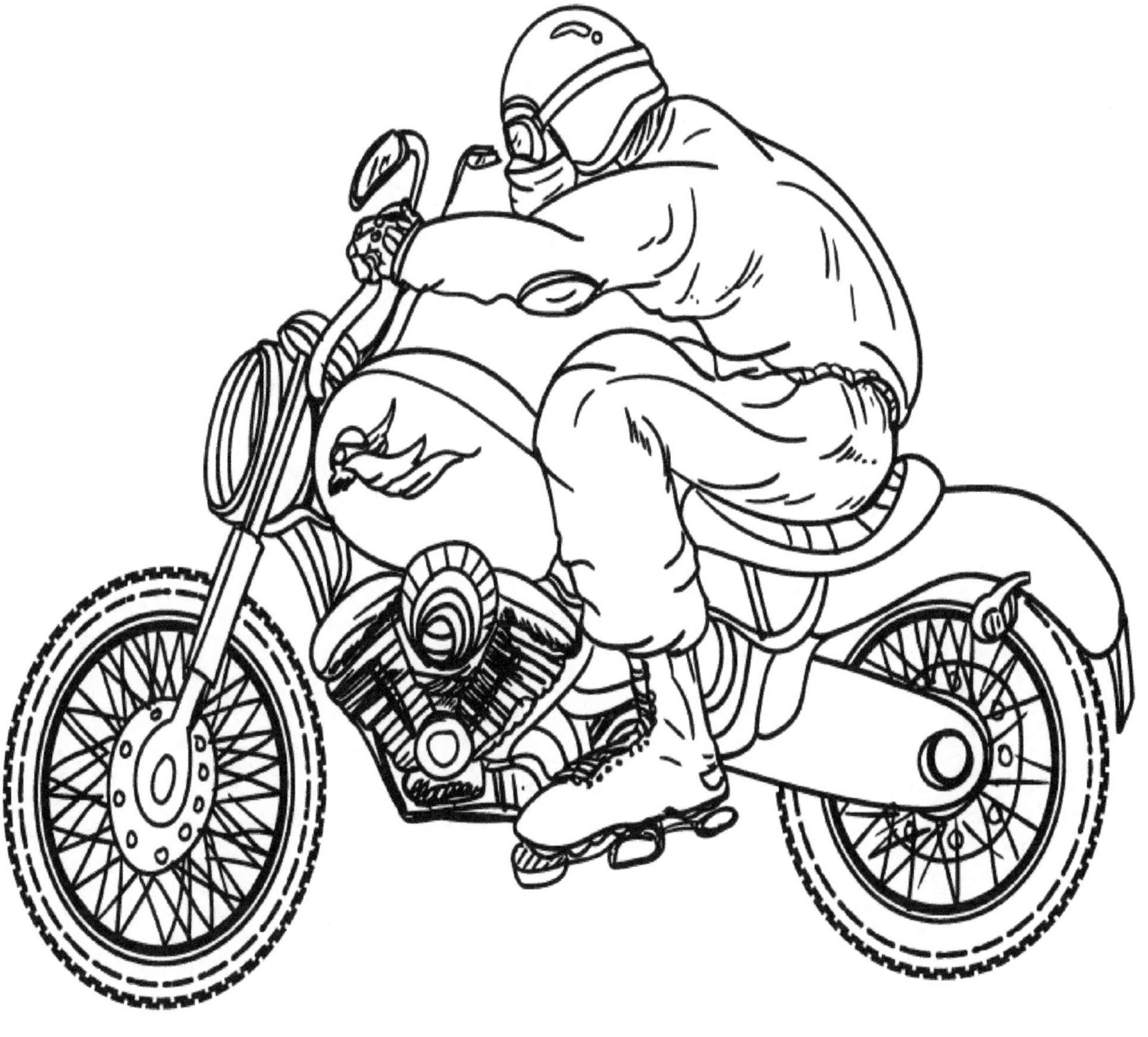

www.ingramcontent.com/pod-product-compliance
Lightning Source LLC
LaVergne TN
LVHW080735120125
801049LV00038B/1127